Gary's Hope

by Gary Hope

"*Gary's Hope*," by Gary Hope. ISBN 978-1-62137-403-9.

Published 2013 by Virtualbookworm.com Publishing Inc., P.O. Box 9949, College Station, TX 77842, US. ©2013, Gary Hope. All rights reserved. No part of this publication may be reproduced, stored in a retrieval system, or transmitted in any form or by any means, electronic, mechanical, recording or otherwise, without the prior written permission of Gary Hope.

Manufactured in the United States of America.

1
Lord, I've Got a Problem . . . ME

This book is about some extraordinary people I've known, with some interesting (or not) facts and stories thrown in. Everything I'm writing about is true, to the best of my knowledge; however, it wouldn't surprise me if some of the men and women in these accounts will try to downplay their actual roles . . . which is understandable, due to the passage of time—which tends to blur our memories to some extent. And, because they probably think that their lives are so very normal and that they themselves are not noteworthy of any attention . . . I beg to differ.

I'm starting with a story I found to be fascinating as a whole and pretty amazing broken down into each facet. It starts with a young man born around 1893 I think; he had never been away from his home in southeastern North

Carolina until he joined the Army during World War 1 and was sent to France to preserve our freedom fighting the aggressive and determined Germans (determined to once again unleash their fury on their neighbors . . . the boastful, arrogant high and mighty French). It's truly a wonder more countries didn't want to fight the French; after all, it was a certain victory fighting them.

I recommend reading a wonderful book called "All Quiet on the Western Front," which gives a dynamic and graphic picture of what men went through during The Great War . . . and it's one of the best books ever written, not just about war, but ever written. The young man in my story—and my hero—was assigned to the front, which meant he was stationed several hundred yards from the German lines. WW1 was characterized by what was termed "trench warfare," which meant each side dug ditches, or trenches, about 6' deep all along the front and charged each other and shot at each other and bombed each other and gassed each other from these trenches. Each time one side advanced a little, new trenches would have to be dug—it was a full time job digging these ditches.

My hero, being strong of back and hard of head , was immediately recruited to dig the trenches. The front lines constantly moved—back and forth depending on the bravery of the Generals back at headquarters; so, new ditches were needed all the time. The very nature of war means no 8 hour days, or 40 hour weeks, consequently, he dug ditches all his waking hours, except when he was required to pick up his rifle and fire at the charging Germans. There were no barracks, no tents, everything had to be below ground level so the Germans couldn't see you and shoot you. That meant my hero, and all those other brave men as well, lived in the ditches 24/7.

He ate all his meals in the ditch, went to the bathroom in the ditch, slept there, fought there, cried there, cursed there and saw many friends and comrades die there. He was gassed (ghastly fogs of poison the Germans lofted in), bombed, machine gunned, and hand-grenaded . . . yet somehow he lived through it all for 13 months. In the winter, there was no way to warm yourself in the trench, no fires were allowed because the Germans could then see the smoke and loft a bomb over; so he, like all of his friends nearly froze to death . . . some did. It was common practice to urinate on your hands just to feel the momentary sensation of warmth on your fingers.

In the summer, all types of vermin inhabited the ditch . . . rats, lice, ticks, fleas and many unnamed and unknown other creatures that made their lives all the more miserable . . . if death and terror weren't enough! However, our hero survived it all (physically) and made it back home—a miracle in and of itself. From this time in his life until the end of his life he was reluctant to discuss what happened in those ditches; it was all too terrible to conjure up those thoughts again. Sudden loud noises, firecrackers, cars backfiring, or a book dropping to the floor always startled him and made him jump—50 years later he was still affected. Things like he experienced don't just go away . . . they stay with you.

But, he made it back to southeastern North Carolina—garden spot of the world, as it is; without a scratch from the war, met a young lady who was described as "sweet as cotton candy" but much prettier and got married. Soon afterwards, he was chopping some wood for the stove and cut off half his big toe; at least it wasn't the Germans who injured him.

My hero lived a fairly normal life, you could say; if you consider raising 6 children during the Great Depression normal. But, just as they are all getting used to "normal," those crazy Germans are at it again. This time, it's not just the surrendering French, they also invade Poland, Belgium, Czechoslovakia and any other country their insanely, demonic Fuhrer tells them to. Finally, after the Japanese made the HUGE mistake of attacking us, we entered WW II. They should've let the sleeping dog lie, because when they woke us . . . it was OVER for them and their German buddies. It was only a matter of time before we settled the score; unfortunately, tens of millions of people lost their lives because of this insanity.

Seemingly, DNA from our hero was passed along to his children and during this latest World War his three oldest sons joined the military (the youngest son wasn't of age, he had to wait until the Korean War to join up). And to cover all their bases . . . one joined the Army, one joined the Marines and one joined the Navy . . . off to war they went. My first story is of the son who was sent to France, just like his father, to fight the dastardly Germans (again) and save the homeland of the white flag waving French. Unfortunately for him, his arrival in France was on D-Day, June 6, 1944 parachuting behind German lines in the early morning total darkness of that fateful day.

The Germans, who were crazy but not stupid, knew we were coming, they just weren't sure where and when . . . but they were ready and they were waiting for us. Our hero was in the Airborne, not very fortunate for him, a dangerous occupation at the time. It was decided by the Generals again, who were planning everything from merry, old England, that the invasion would start before daylight, so our hero, along with thousands of other heroes would parachute inland after the initial artillery barrage. Jumping from an airplane is dangerous in and of itself; try jumping in total darkness , behind enemy lines, being shot at, not knowing where you would land, nor what you would do if you even made the landing alive—which many didn't.

Soldiers were landing in trees, breaking legs and arms; landing in lakes and rivers drowning; landing on houses full of Germans and being killed summarily . . . it was a terrible, terrible scene. Our hero couldn't see anything until the ground whacked him when he landed—he could only hear the bullets whizzing by him as the Germans were firing blindly at them. He didn't know where he was, nor how far it was back to the beach where all the other Americans were. The Americans were given little "clickers," so they could click each other to let the other know he was an American . . . the problem was that the Germans stole the clickers from the dead GI's and now everybody had clickers! There was no way to know who was friendly or hostile in the dark, French countryside.

His orders were to make it to the beach and help with the invasion . . . and that's what he did. Eventually, after sun up he slowly made it through the bullets and the bombs to the beach where the Allies were landing. There was still heavy fighting on the beach front and it was a horribly expensive landing in terms of human lives lost . . . just horrible. Our hero, like his Dad before him, is hesitant to bring up those memories from the depths of his mind—I can understand that. The only time I ever heard him talk about it was the one scene that he can't get over, one that has haunted him for over 60 years; when he finally made it to the beach, they had all the bodies and body parts of the men who had died that day stacked up like cordwood all along the beach front; rows and rows of them—he has never been able to suppress that sight from his mind; it's the image he sees when he closes his eyes at night . . . 60 some years later.

The next son (and brother) was also in WWII, but he joined the Marines . . . Lord only knows why. He was shipped off to the Pacific where we were fighting the Japanese at the time. Funny how time changes things . . . today, the Japanese and Germans are our great friends and economic allies and we love them—well, I think we do. But not back in 1944 and 1945 when our second brother was on an island in the Pacific where there was a terrible battle raging. His Marine platoon was in danger of being overrun one horrible day . . . Japanese troops surrounding them; withering machine gun fire, mortar fire, and tank fire had them pinned down hopelessly.

Suddenly, a Japanese tank starts motoring directly at our lines, with the intention of wiping them out once and for all. My hero in this story leaps over some fallen comrades, grabs a bazooka, runs out in the open to get a clear shot and fires his bazooka at point blank range making a direct hit, blowing up the tank and all those around it who were following on foot. This action so startled the Japanese and so emblazoned the Americans that it turned the tide completely in that battle. The Marines took the offensive and eventually secured the island. Our hero was awarded the "Silver Star" for bravery above and beyond the call of duty; for saving untold American lives at no thought of his own. However, he never told his story. It was only known from those who witnessed it and recommended him for the medal and award. When he got home after the war, he never mentioned it, never even told his family he had earned the medal.

Like his Dad before him and his brother, he never talked about those events which are too traumatic to relive. Fortunately, we were able to find out about these brave, heroic men and what they did for our country . . . there is no way to appropriately thank them for their service, their bravery, courage and will. We all will be indebted to them and hundreds of thousands of others just like them forever.

The third son chose to join the Navy and served his country in the Pacific during the war; even though I've asked him about his experiences on ships fighting the Japanese, he just sluffs it off saying he really didn't do anything special and was just one of many onboard the ship. But, what more would I have expected him to say, knowing where he came from.

The first hero was my grandfather, Grover Cleveland Townsend and his wife Ida Elizabeth Townsend (sweet as cotton candy) who my sister and niece are named after. Their sons, my uncle, Earl Townsend was our paratrooper; our Marine was my uncle G.C. Townsend and our sailor was my uncle Paul Townsend. I'm still hoping some of their incredible DNA has filtered down to me . . . however, I've yet to see it manifest itself in any credible form—but I've got a few years left hopefully. What I do know, is that it's there; maybe below the surface sitting latently, waiting for the opportune time; I hope I'm as brave as these men when the time comes.

G.C. and Ida Elizabeth Townsend

2

"If everyone's thinking the same way, then someone isn't thinking."

General Patton

My sister loves shopping at Wal-Mart . . . Loves it! I personally don't get it, but obviously a lot of people do, because the parking lots at Wal-Marts are full nearly all the time. I recently found some interesting statistics about Wal-Mart that I'd like to share:

Americans spend $36,000,000 at Wal-Mart every hour of every day . . . again, that's every hour of every day!

This works out to $20,928 profit every MINUTE!

Wal-Mart will sell more from January 1 to St. Patrick's Day (March 17) than Target sells all year.

Wal-Mart is bigger than Home Depot + Kroger + Target + Sears + Costco + K-Mart all combined.

Wal-Mart employs 1.6 million people, is the world's largest private employer, and most employees speak English.

Wal-Mart is the largest company in the history of the world.

Wal-Mart started selling food only 15 years ago and now sells more than Kroger and Safeway combined; and during this same period, 31 big supermarket chains sought bankruptcy.

Wal-Mart now sells more food than any other store in the world.

Wal-Mart has approximately 3,900 stores in the USA, which is 1,000 more than it had five years ago.

This year about 7.2 billion purchases will be made at Wal-Mart. (Earth's population is about 6.5 billion)

90% of all Americans live within 15 miles of a Wal-Mart.

Now, ask yourself this question: who would you rather run our country? Politicians, who have no practical experience in anything, except being politicians; or the President of Wal-Mart who absolutely knows how to run things, make a profit, grow, expand and serve the country?

Nothing is broken at Wal-Mart . . . everything runs very efficiently and effectively; whereas in our country today:

The Post Office is broken and nearly bankrupt

Social Security is teetering

Fannie Mae is a mess

Medicare and Medicaid are so convoluted and messed up, I don't think anyone understands them

The Department of Energy (created in 1977 to lessen our dependence on foreign oil) has ballooned to 16,000 employees with a budget of $24 Billion and we now import more oil than ever.

Everything seems broken and we can't seem to help our own Seniors, Veterans, Orphans and Homeless; yet we can provide aid to Haiti, Chili, Japan, Turkey, Pakistan, etc., etc. etc . . .

Now, our politicians want to FREEZE Social Security payments (money we've all paid in over the course of our working lives by the way), yet they have voted themselves a pay raise in 2013!

Democrats . . . Republicans . . . Tea Party . . . Libertarians? No, no, no and no . . . give me the president of Wal-Mart to run our country and lets' get things moving again!

3

"What I'm looking for isn't out there ... it's in me.

Helen Keller

Ever feel useless? Abandoned? Lonely? Worthless? We all do. . . . We all do. Ever ask why I'm here? What is my purpose? What am I supposed to do? Have you ever wondered how anyone, including God, could use me for anything worthwhile? Even the famous and beautiful people have deep periods of loneliness and self doubt. John Lennon always questioned his worthiness and suffered depression, Madonna has asked the question "Why am I here?" Kurt Cobain was so disgusted and tormented with his life that he blew his brains out. This list goes on and on and on. . . . The rehab facilities in California and elsewhere are PACKED with the rich and famous . . . why?

One of the most beautiful women in Hollywood, Halle Berry says "Being thought of as a beautiful woman has spared me nothing in life. Not heartache, not trouble, love has been difficult, beauty is essentially meaningless and it's always transitory."

Albert Einstein said "It is strange to be known so universally, and yet be so lonely."

We all have a "hole" in our hearts, yearning for something, for a relationship with our creator. Drugs can't fill that void, drink can't, relationships can't, not power nor money nor any other worldly thing. That's why the rehab centers are all filled up, people are looking in all the wrong places to fill the void in their lives and in their hearts. We were made by God, and for God; and until we figure that out, life isn't going to make sense. But don't be disheartened, God loves you and wants you to be happy; He can always use you, no matter how broken you think you might be. Just look at a few of the people throughout history God has used:

Noah was a drunk

Abraham was too old

Isaac was a daydreamer

Jacob was a liar

Leah was ugly

Joseph was abused

Moses had a stuttering problem

Gideon was afraid

Samson had long hair and was a womanizer

Rahab was a prostitute

Jeremiah and Timothy were too young

David had an affair and was a murderer

Elijah was suicidal

Isaiah preached naked

Jonah ran from God

Naomi was a widow

Job went bankrupt

Peter denied Christ. . . . 3 times!

The disciples fell asleep while praying

Martha worried about Everything

The Samaritan woman was divorced more than once.

Zaccheus was too small

Paul was too religious

Timothy had an ulcer . . .

AND

Lazarus was DEAD!

No more excuses . . . God can use you to your full potential. There is no key to happiness, the door is always open. Faith is the ability to not panic. And always remember, God loves you and He will never forget you nor forsake you. He promised us that . . . and He always keeps His promises.

4

"The definition of a bore is someone who, when asked how they are feeling, will actually tell you."

Ruth Graham

And now, the definition of a "good man" . . . Alfred Paul Townsend. My uncle, my hero and one of the stars of my first story about WWII . . . Uncle Paul was the brother who joined the Navy. However, anyone could join the Navy, not everyone can be a model husband, father, son, brother and Christian man. Not perfect, he never could adequately correct that hook he had with his driver . . . just a good man.

After the war Uncle Paul and a friend of his went on a double date with two young ladies from Robeson county, so you know they had to be beauties . . . and they were. The problem was that Uncle Paul was attracted to his friend's date a lot more than to his own date. Not one to let a friendship get in the way of a budding romance,

Uncle Paul and the young lady quickly let it be known they wanted to switch dates—I think at Aunt Dot's urging, but that may be in question. However, they quickly became an item and married forthwith and Uncle Paul had now done exactly like his Dad had done years ago and found him a wife as sweet as sugar cane; but you know, sugar cane can be a tad spicy if not harvested in time—and so it was with Aunt Dot. A little spice to keep the recipe healthy. After moves to Florence (not the one in Italy) and Chicago for schooling, they settled in Charlotte and raised three beautiful , intelligent children. Seemingly pretty normal stuff for the 1950's and 60's.

I first stated that this book was not about me, and it's not; but a little background information is needed to fully understand Uncle Paul's life. I was living in the best little town in America at the time, about a 3 hour drive from Charlotte in the days of two-lane traffic. I lived with my mom and sister and grandparents, no dad—a later story, maybe. Uncle Paul would make the drive from Charlotte to Red Springs once a month, packing up his three kids and come to visit his mom and dad and be a surrogate father to me. I don't know why he took an interest in me, but he did; maybe it was just carry over love he had for his sister—my mom.

Uncle Paul would play catch with me in the yard and talk to me about things—it was nice getting advice and lessons from a man; I really loved that. But what I loved even more was that Uncle Paul would take me golfing! Just me and him, oh how exciting that was; later, when his son Ronnie was old enough, he would come along as well. I didn't mind sharing Uncle Paul with Ronnie. I had a driver, 3 iron, 7 iron, 9 iron and putter and the advice and attention of someone I admired and loved. Uncle Paul was a golfer, he actually knew what he was doing . . . I didn't have a clue; he taught me everything, or at least tried to. I'm pretty sure I was a knucklehead most of the time; I'll never understand how he had the patience to walk 18 holes with me trying to teach me about life and golf. But nearly every 3-4 weeks, he came, we played, he taught and I learned. He didn't have to do any of that, he was just a good man.

Years later, after my grandparents had passed away, and my Mom and sister and me were basically alone, Uncle Paul and Aunt Dot would invite us to spend Christmas with them at their home in Charlotte with their family so we wouldn't be alone. I'm sure this wasn't their optimal Christmas fantasy . . . having a goofy teenager like me and a petulant, moody younger teenager like my sister spend Christmas at your house. But they did it.

On and on through the years Uncle Paul always did the right thing, arranged family reunions, visited those who were sick, went to weddings and funerals when none of the rest of us wanted to. He did all the things you wished you would have done . . . but didn't. And all through his life, up till present day, I've never . . . NEVER heard him say a four letter word, nor an unkind word about anyone for any reason; and I'm sure he's probably lost his temper from time to time—I told you he wasn't perfect—but I've never seen it. Now, Aunt Dot . . . let's just say she will tell it like it is—and I respect that.

If you remember my story about WWII, you'll recall Uncle Paul's brother, G.C., who joined the Marines and won the Silver Star. After the war Uncle G.C. married and had 6 kids, it was tough providing for a large family, but he provided just fine. . . . nothing fancy or wistful, just a man providing for his growing family. Uncle Paul, knowing the financial constraints of such a large family, always made certain that each of the kids received special Christmas presents. And checked on them throughout the year, helping when he could and should. He left a lasting impression on that family, one that resulted in one of Uncle G.C.'s kids, Kenny, naming his son after Uncle Paul. Enough said.

Finally, the last thing I'm going to write about (this book isn't big enough to list all I should say about Uncle Paul), is what he did for his other sister, my Aunt Mary. Her health had deteriorated to the point of leg amputations and heart attacks which made it necessary for her to reside in a Rest Home in King, N.C. She recently passed away, but for the entire time she was in the rest home (6-8 years, I don't remember), Uncle Paul and Aunt Dot would drive from Charlotte to King every week to visit her, bring her food, take her on short trips . . . everything you wished you had done for Aunt Mary, but didn't. Just fighting the Charlotte traffic is daunting itself, and being in your 80's as he and Aunt Dot are, making that drive every week to see his sister . . . Have you ever spent time in a rest home visiting? I could make it about 30 minutes, sometimes 45 minutes on my visits to see Aunt Mary . . . they stayed all day. I don't understand how they did that, I don't understand the innate goodness of those two people.

So, now you have the definition of a "good man."

Uncle Paul

5

"Life is tough. . . . it's even tougher if you're stupid."

John Wayne

I don't have a pet, sometimes I wish I did, except the times when you have to walk them, or clean up their poop, or spend a lot of money at the vet. . . . other than that, I think I'd like having a pet; a dog for sure, not a cat—definitely not a cat. However, if you're a young unmarried man looking for a wife, you might want to read this list of 13 reasons dogs are better than women . . . and for clarity, they are NOT my reasons, just something I read on the internet:

1. The later you come home, the more excited they are to see you.
2. Dogs will forgive you for playing with other dogs.
3. If your dog is gorgeous, other dogs won't hate it.
4. A dog's disposition stays the same all month long.

5. Dogs like it if you leave a lot of things on the floor.
6. A dog's parents never visit
7. Dogs don't notice if you call them by another dog's name.
8. Dogs don't hate their bodies.
9. Dogs seldom outlive you
10. Dogs can't talk.
11. You never have to wait on a dog; they are ready 24 / 7
12. Another man will seldom steal your dog
13. If a dog leaves, it won't take half of your stuff.

6

"I skate to where the puck is going to be, not where it has been."

Wayne Gretzky

A little known statistic about WAGES

Salary of retired US Presidents $450,000 for life

Salary of House/ Senate members $174,000 for life

Salary of Speaker of the House $223,500 for life

Salary of Majority/ Minority leaders $193,400 for life

Average salary of a soldier deployed in Afghanistan . . . $38,000

Average income for seniors on Social Security . . . $12,000

Does this make you feel bad? It does me. So here are some items to keep you going, read these and as Jimmy V said . . ."Don't give up, don't ever give up."

The author John Grisham had his first book rejected 28 times.

Frank Woolworth was told he "didn't have enough common sense" to serve customers

Michael Jordon was cut from his high school basketball team

Thomas Edison failed 2000 times to invent the first incandescent light bulb . . . he said he that had found 1,999 ways "not to do it."

Woody Allen flunked film school class and was thrown out of college

Marilyn Monroe was told "You'd better learn secretarial work or else get married," you'll never make it.

Elvis Presley was told "You ain't going nowhere son . . . you ought to go back to driving a truck."

Babe Ruth also broke the major league record for strikeouts.

Malcolm Forbes failed to make his school's newspaper staff.

And finally . . .

General Douglas MacArthur was rejected from West Point not once, but twice!

Keep your chin up, keep plugging away, have faith in yourself . . . you'll be okay.

7

"Most folks are as happy as they make their minds up to be."

Abraham Lincoln

Another special man I want to write about is my cousin, Herbert Grady Fowler, Jr. Or Joe, as we all knew him; if you were named Herbert Grady, you'd want to be called Joe as well. I say we knew him, because he's no longer with us; Joe died about 35 years ago at the age of 36 . . . I still miss him terribly.

Joe was 7 years older than me and a true hero in my eyes . . . I wanted to be like him, good athlete, good looking and fun to be around. I lived with Joe and his mom, my Aunt Mary and Uncle Herbert for two years; first grade and then again in the fifth grade. My mom was living in Virginia at the time and couldn't afford child care for both me and my sister, so I lived with Aunt Mary and Joe and Uncle Herbert those two years. So, when I was in 5th grade, Joe was a senior in high school—I was very impressed. We would all go to his baseball and football games, he was a star on both; I remember after one football game Aunt Mary asked him why he received a penalty for "unsportsmanlike conduct" during the game. He gave an obscure answer , she didn't like his answer and told him so and Joe said "Bull Hockey!" Scared me to death . . . I'd never heard language like that, I thought for sure Uncle Herbert would beat Joe and spank me just for hearing that kind of talk. But, it passed and I learned a new saying to impress my friends with . . ."Bull Hockey."

Joe would come home from practice and prop his feet up and offer to pay me 25 cents to wipe the dirt from between his toes. Disgusting I know . . . but think about it. . . . baseball cards were a penny a piece then, and for doing this nasty deed, I could get 25 baseball cards! It was a GREAT deal for me.

After school he joined the Air Force, something in the DNA of these Townsend's that makes them all want to join the military. He spent a year or so in Germany during his tenure and returned home to start his life. He married the lovely Sara Petty and settled down in King, NC.

They came to visit us often in Red Springs and one time in particular was very memorable for us all. I had a broken down hippie van with a bed in the back that I bought for $100, but it wouldn't run good; Joe volunteered to repair it for me. Great! I went out and did what young guys do and returned home that evening to find my white van completely blackened . . . BLACKENED! What was going on? In trying to repair the van and taking it on a test drive, it somehow caught fire and burned up—don't ask me how. All I know is that it cost me another $50 to have someone tow my $100 van to the junk yard. Joe did feel bad, and I felt worse for him.

He and Sara took me in twice in my life when I had nowhere else to go and no money to go with . . . Boarded me, fed me and put up with my moody nonsense. I'm certain I was not the ideal tenant. But they did it and my admiration for my hero cousin only grew . . . I really loved that man.

He was a little overweight, just a little . . . and with the heart issues in our family his doctor urged him to quit smoking and lose some weight. With Sara's help, he did just that, sort of. He was a good dieter, but also a good cheater. At that time we all had season tickets to Wake Forest basketball games and would go together. Before we left home, Joe would eat his dietary meal and drink a diet Coke. Then at the game he and I would "go to the bathroom," which was really the excuse he needed to go the hot dog stand, order two dogs and INHALE them in no time flat! Of course this was the secret between us that he thought no one else knew . . . but I always had the feeling Sara knew what was going on.

Anyway, one day he and Sara were driving down the road and Joe says "something's wrong" and passes out while driving. Somehow, Sara gets the car over to the side of the road, but she knows he's gone. Massive heart attack, too sudden, too soon, too agonizing, too . . . everything.

My hero is gone.

Joe

8

"Any man who thinks he can be happy and prosperous by letting the American government take care of him, better take a closer look at the American Indian."

Henry Ford

When it all feels broken

When you're tired of hoping

When nobody's listening

When you're tired of giving

Keep your heart wide open and Love Anyway.

When there's nothing certain

When your heart is hurting

When your world is empty

When you just feel lonely

Keep yourself wide open and Love Anyway.

When your faith gets shaken

Once your love gets taken

When the field comes at you

And the odds are all against you

Keep your arms wide open and Love Anyway.

Anyway you can, everything you have

Even when it hurts so bad . . . Love Anyway

9

"God loves you because of who God is, not because of anything you did or didn't do."

I'm going to write about a few friends of mine, in no particular order. They are all good and great men, fathers, sons, brothers and terrific friends. It's hard for me to think of one of them without thinking of all of them; we've been tethered together throughout our lives now for 50 + years. I think it's pretty unusual to have even one or two friends who last that long . . . I've got five; I am truly blessed.

Some background on these "boys," as I'll refer to them; first, we all LOVED sports and played all sports with and against each other from our earliest memories to the lies we tell now about how good we used to be. And most of us went to the First Baptist Church together, Sunday School together and sat in the back row and giggled together—until our mom's would give us the evil eye. I used to think it was sports that bound us together . . . basketball, sandlot football, tennis, golf,

Ping-Pong, softball and especially baseball—oh, how we did love that game. From our earliest Little League games, where we'd jump in our uniforms at 11:00 in the morning for a 6:00 game that night—it was so exciting and so much fun.

However, the more I examine our friendship—which goes on to this day—I think it's more psychological or emotional than any of us realized then, or even now. All of us, of course, grew up in the same town, went to the same school and had the same friends, some outside our little circle and some not and even dated a lot of the same girls—that really depends on whose stories you tend to believe the most. But, the X-factor (in my humble Freudian mind) is that even though some of us had sisters, not one of us had a brother . . . not one of the 6 of us had a brother—so, subconsciously, we became each other's brothers by default. Which tends to creep me out a little since I've just recently learned that several of my so-called brothers actually DATED my sister! Now that's just not right . . . luckily, none of them married her, so there's no incest involved, or we'd really have a problem . . . baseball or no baseball.

We've all traveled together, been to countless ballgames (high school, college and professional), been in each other's weddings, seen kids born, been to mom's and dad's funerals and other friend's funerals; commiserated through hard times, prayed for each other during illnesses and sicknesses, been saddened by divorces and through it all, through it all . . . we've always had each other, knowing you could always count on your friends for solace, guidance, comfort and companionship.

Now, I'd like to write a little about each of these boys . . . as I said earlier, in no particular order—one is not more important than another; although one or two may be handsomer than some of us, and in one case, even smarter than some of us, still . . . we're all the same . . . you'll see.

The Friends All Together

10

"No one is in charge of your happiness but you!"

First, Larry, I won't use last names, they know who they are and this way I can't be sued for defamation of character. Larry's first because, well . . . .he's the shortest and he needs a boost sometimes. He grew up with a built in disadvantage, he lived directly across the street from the school, making it nearly impossible to play hooky without being noticed—a terrible burden to suffer. His dad ran a small , community grocery store, which employed several of Larry's friends from time to time . . . however, I'm sure Larry's dad was hesitant to hire any of these young bucks around World Series time or ACC tournament time. Afterall, priorities were priorities and if the decision was listening to the radio when Mickey Mantle was at bat or Van Williford was attempting a foul shot that could beat Carolina . . . well, you do the math.

I always looked up to Larry, not in a literal sense (he was always short), but figuratively. He always seemed like he was a better student than the rest of us, more serious than the rest of us, way more religious than us and dated prettier girls than us. Our preacher, Mr. Mattox , loved him . . . well he loved a little less after Larry broke Mr. Mattox's hand throwing a ball too hard at him, but he still loved him. In fact, it was Mr. Mattox who drove Larry to Wake Forest University one day to get him enrolled—preacher's pet.

There were times I wanted to swat him away like a nit or a pest, these were when he guarded me too closely in basketball or sandlot football. He was so quick you couldn't get away from him and it would irritate me that he guarded me so close. I wanted to just push him away and curse him—but, it was Larry and you simply couldn't say things like "bull hockey" around Larry . . . no, you couldn't do that. And let me tell you another thing, don't EVER let him tackle you in sandlot football . . . run out of bounds, fall down, call time out—-anything! Just don't let him tackle you, he played as if HE was wearing shoulder pads and a helmet and you weren't.

Well, he eventually graduated (though he never got any taller) and enrolled at Wake Forest and since he was a year ahead of us in school, we high school seniors were duly impressed. We went up to visit him occasionally and attend a losing Wake Forest football game, and it was all great fun and further enhanced our already lofty impression of our friend. I was wondering if he would take Mr. Mattox's place as our preacher when he graduated . . . imagine that, one of our friends as our preacher . . . Just think of the sins we could then get away with!

But, Larry came home from college. And, he wasn't Larry anymore . . . not by a long shot. Oh, he was still short, but he was smoking (SMOKING!!!) and I even heard a four letter word—I truly did. Yes, our friend, our role model, our counselor had turned into one of us. I can only blame it on the dastardly and despicable Yankees he was forced to room with at Wake Forest; how could he possibly resist all they exposed him to . . . it was totally unfair. Cigarettes, adult beverages, four- letter words and the newly created Whopper . . . and, he had become a cheerleader. Yes my friends, our long lost companion had become a cheerleader at Wake Forest (I'm pretty sure it was only to get better seats at basketball games), the sad part being he seldom had anything good to cheer about . . . such is life.

Well, we progress . . . after a dangerous car wreck on McRacken's curve in Kernersville, he settled into the academic world and did an admirable job for someone so short. After a few minor setbacks, he settled into the family life as well and he and his wife Lynn have reared two great kids and are helping rear two great grandkids. He's a wonderful family man, he's a great dad and he's a great granddad and I'm proud to call him my friend.

Although he initially entered Wake Forest with divinity as his goal, things changed; questions were raised, and questions were answered. He and I have had some serious discussions about religion and faith, which are between him and me . . . but I cherish those talks and always regard his views with the utmost esteem.

These days, he loves to come visit Winston-Salem and his old school, Wake Forest—truth be known, he'd love to start school there all over again. Although a 60 some year old cheerleader might get some second looks, he could probably still fit in with the incoming freshman class, freshmen are the short ones aren't they? Foothills,

Finnegan's, Firebirds, Diamondback Grill, Chelsea's, Hutch & Harris, Village Tavern . . . he loves them all and we do enjoy each other's company.

I'm proud to call him my friend, he's what a lot of us would like to be when we grow up. A very good man. But, don't ever . . . ever let him tackle you.

Larry

//
"Forgive everyone, everything."

Trivia

It has been calculated that in the last 3,500 years , there have only been 230 years of peace throughout the "civilized" world.

The total number of Americans killed in the Civil War is greater than the combined total of Americans killed in all other wars.

In 1920 for the first time in recorded history, the average life expectancy of human beings exceeded that of goldfish. Before that year, a newborn infant could expect to live 48.4 years. The goldfish had a life span of over 50.

The average life span of a peasant during the medieval ages was 25 years.

In 1980 the city of Detroit presented Saddam Hussein with a key to the city.

There are 92 known cases of nuclear bombs lost at sea.

Harry S. Truman was the last U.S. President with no college degree . . . is that relevant? Well, read the following facts about Mr. Truman and you be the judge:

The only asset he had when he died was the house he lived in, in Independence, Missouri. His wife had inherited the house from her mother and other than their years in the White House, they lived their entire lives there.

When he retired from office in 1952, his income was a U.S. Army pension of $13,507 a year. Congress, noting that he was paying for his own stamps, granted him an "allowance" and later a pension of $25,000 per year.

After President Eisenhower was inaugurated, Harry and Bess drove home to Missouri by themselves. No Secret Service following them.

When offered corporate positions at large salaries, he declined, stating "You don't want me. You want the office of the President, and that doesn't belong to me. It belongs to the American people and it's not for sale."

As President he paid for all of his own travel expenses and food.

Good old Harry Truman was correct when he observed, "My choices in life were either to be a piano player in a whore house or a politician. And to tell the truth, there's hardly any difference!"

Let's dig him up and clone him!

Susan, President Truman and Casey

12

"In America, anyone can be President—that's the problem."

George Carlin

My next friend I'm going to say a little about is my good buddy Bill. Another great and good man. My friend is currently experiencing a serious health concern, but he's a fighter and he has prayers from many, many people on his side. Bill also went to Wake Forest and was there at the same time my sister was there. Now, understand this; Bill and my sister grew up a block apart in a town of 4,000 people . . . his sister and my sister were good buddies. They went to the same schools and the same church—they were well acquainted. However, my sister swears she never saw Bill at Wake Forest and to this day does not believe he actually went there. I don't understand this and I'm staying out of it.

After graduation from Wake (or wherever he went), Bill chose a path in city/ county government and was a town manager for his entire career . . . most of it as the city manager of Cary, N.C. Bill's main quality is he's a devoted baseball fan, he pulls for the Dodgers, but we can overlook that. What is most striking about the character of my friend is his unique ability to work in civil government with mayors, police chiefs, town councilmen (and women), and various other political cronies and hacks. In his position, he truly must be cognizant of the realities of saying the right thing, or the wrong thing at the most inopportune times. Being politically correct and taking the middle of the road approach, without stepping on too may toes must have been next to impossible to do . . . but he did it and did it well.

He was such a driving force in the town of Cary, he spearheaded the movement for the town to bid for and win the right to build the Baseball USA complex in Cary. A magnificent facility of several diamonds and the place where our USA Olympic team trains and plays. Bill was so important that the complex is named "William B. Coleman Field," in his honor. We recently went there with Bill to see the USA national team play the Cuban national team and received the royal treatment since we were there with the namesake of the stadium.

Bill, obviously, knew how to play the political game and play it very, very well. What none of us can understand is HOW he did that??? We know Bill, on any subject, he's either black or white; all or none; yes or no; good or bad . . . there is no gray area with Bill—and he's very passionate about his feelings. He doesn't only like women's field hockey, he LOVES women's field hockey. He doesn't just not like Carolina . . . he hates Carolina (which is understandable). If you want to know how he feels about something, all you have to do is ask him . . . just be sure you really want to know, because he will tell you in no uncertain terms.

Another of Bill's great qualities is that he had a gorgeous sister, well he actually had several sisters, but only one in our grade in school . . . Tana. She was every boys dream date, just that none of us were dreamy enough to date her. The closest I ever came was playing her in ping pong one day at recreation in the summertime . . . and I'm counting that! Bill's dad got a new job in Greensboro when Bill was a senior in high school and they moved there; sad day for our town—losing a beauty like Tana. However, somehow my mom arranged for us to move into Bill's old house, which was obviously vacant now. Since my sister was at Wake Forest, I got my choice of bedrooms . . . guess which one I chose? Yep, I was now sleeping in Tana Coleman's bedroom; I, Gary Hope, was actually sleeping and reading and dressing and playing records in Tana Coleman's bedroom . . . dream come true!

As with Larry, Bill is a great dad—one of the best ever. He and his son Ben have been on such cool trips; ball games, hunting, vacations . . . but most importantly, Bill is there for Ben, spending time talking, listening, just being a dad, being Ben's hero. That's the most important thing. Ben is one lucky dude to have a dad like Bill. And I'm lucky to call him my friend.

Bill

13

"If at first you don't succeed, try doing it the way mom told you to in the beginning."

A survey was done in China and the three best-known western names were: Jesus Christ, Richard Nixon and Elvis Presley. 2 out of 3 ain't bad.

The reason Julius Caesar wore a laurel wreath on his head was to cover the onset of baldness . . . I totally understand.

The house where Thomas Jefferson wrote the Declaration of Independence was replaced with a hamburger stand.

Sir Winston Churchill rationed himself to 15 cigars and 1 quart of whiskey a day.

Lady Astor once told Winston Churchill "if you were my husband, I would poison your coffee." His reply . . . "if you were my wife, I would drink it."

England's Queen Anne (1665-1714) outlived all 17 of her children

Mozart never went to school

34% of the American adult population is overweight, according to the US Surgeon General's office; and , after smoking, weight related conditions are the 2cd leading cause of death in the USA.

Only 8% of Americans are getting the amount of exercise recommended for minimal health benefits.

China and India produce more peanuts than the United States does . . . really? Yes.

It takes 540 peanuts to make a 12 oz jar of peanut butter

An average American child eats 1,500 peanut butter and jelly sandwiches before graduating from high school.

Sharks are the only animals that never get sick. They are immune to every known disease including cancer.

14

"God is never in a hurry, but He's always on time."

My friend Allen is one of the smartest people I know, definitely the smartest baseball trivia man alive. If somehow you were ever curious what Bill "Moose" Skowron hit in 1959, you don't need to Google it, just ask Allen—-he'll know. What was Whitey Ford's record in 1962? What was the Dodgers starting lineup in 1966? He knows all that stuff, plus he can name the Platters 5 biggest hits and tell you where Otis Redding went to high school and who Jim Morrison took to the senior prom . . . I guarantee it!

Allen and his dad would sit on their front porch each summer evening and listen to baseball games on the radio (the best way to enjoy baseball without actually being there). Not just listen, but study the game, take notes, live the game, virtually "be" at Yankee Stadium or Forbes Field or Wrigley Field while physically still residing in rural Robeson County. Best of both worlds. A lot of us listened and watched those games, but Allen memorized those games and all the statistics that went with them. He simply had a knack for remembering things and still does . . . 50 years later, he can tell us who he dated one June evening in 1965, where they went and if he got a goodnight kiss from the young lady—knowing Allen, I'm sure he did. Fortunately, he is just about the only friend of mine who claims not to have dated my sister! And she confirms this, saying they were only "friends," which I always found pretty strange because Allen was just about the biggest hound out there—if you know what I mean.

His exploits with the women are well known in the parking lot of Hardee's in Pembroke, the back alleys of St. Pauls, John's and Alvin's gas stations and various other dirt roads and shady meeting places. Most of the rest of us were not nearly as successful with the young ladies as Allen was, but he was two years older than me, so he had a head start. We would be sitting around the service station late at night , talking about ball games, or girls we'd like to date and here comes Allen driving up after his evening with one of Robeson County's most available young ladies. He didn't have to tell us how the night went . . . we could tell by how wrinkled his shirt was. If it was still starched and pressed, he had an average night . . . but if was all wrinkled up . . . we were in for some good stories!

Allen may also be one of the most competitive people I've known (outside of myself obviously). Didn't matter what sport we played, he would literally fight you in order to win. His goal was to always "shoot the moon" at hearts, or spades , or whatever it was we played late at night in Boots Parris's upstairs apartment—he had to win; but so did I—it sometimes got very interesting. You would never think one of your best friends would want to fight you, but try fouling him while he was attempting a jump shot—and NOT calling the foul. OH MAMA . . . it was on then. But, that was all temporary, when the game was over . . . it was over; we would still ride around at night and debate who had the most hits recently: The Doobie Brothers or Credence Clear Water Revival; or who was the best guitar player: Hendrix, Duane Allman or Eric Clapton—that debate may still be raging.

I have several lasting memories of my friend Allen , some I can actually write about: getting locked up together at the beach for "illegally camping " on the ocean front (the policeman did us a favor, we were freezing and he "locked" us up in his own beach cottage—letting us go in the morning with the warning "Don't come back." We didn't.) And the final thing I want to write about is dear to me because it concerns my mom, whom I love and miss every single day now for 26 years. I was my mother's pet, I could virtually do anything and get away with it, whereas my poor little sister paid the price of my mother's fury at times—not without justice I might add. But, the point being, I was the favorite—we all knew that. So , how do I feel when I come home from school or work and my mom is cooking dinner . . . for Allen!?! What's going on with that? Not just my mom, ALL the mom's loved him, he had that quality that made women just want to take care of him . . ." Oh Allen, are you hungry? Let me fix you something . . . do you want something to drink? I'll get it for you." It was maddening! But that was the effect my good buddy had on people . . . if they only knew.

My friend took a few years to finally meet the woman he needed to meet . . . but he did. The lovely Janice was exactly what Allen needed and they were perfect for each other. 35 years of marriage, a beautiful daughter and grandchildren graced their lives. Then, they had an unwelcome visitor that came to stay and would not leave . . . cancer. It's never easy watching the person you love more than anything suffer. Years of treatments, remissions, more treatments, hope, worry, remission . . . the endless cruel cycle in the life of cancer patients. Cancer finally won, Allen could not fight this battle for Janice, could not call a foul, could not punch it in the nose . . . cancer ultimately and tragically won. We grieved for our friend and prayed for him.

It took a while, a good long while; but hope truly does spring eternal . . . it looks as though my buddy has found someone to share time with again. I hope all turns out well—they both deserve the goodness and riches of life. As with Larry and Bill, I am proud and extremely lucky to call this good man my friend.

Allen

15

"I went on a diet for a month, and all I lost was 30 days!"

I read somewhere that Benjamin Franklin, that great American, lobbied for our national bird to be the wild Turkey instead of the Bald Eagle. He was an extremely intelligent man and I'm sure he had some fine reasons for this odd choice—but I'm glad he didn't get his way on this. Eagles are awesome creatures and they have such a significant symbolism for our country. My friend sent me some facts about eagles I'd like to share . . . I was very impressed:

The eagle has the longest life-span of any bird, it can live up to 70 years. But to reach this age, it must make a hard decision when it's around 40. It's long and flexible talons can no longer grab prey and it's long, sharp beak becomes bent. Its wings become heavy, due to the thick feathers, which become stuck together, making it difficult for the eagle to fly. The eagle is then left with two options: die or go through a painful process of change which lasts about 150 days.

The process requires that the eagle fly to its nest, where it then knocks its beak against a rock until it plucks it out. After plucking it out, the eagle will wait for a new beak to grow back and then it will pluck out it's talons as well. When the new talons grow back, the eagle starts plucking out its old-aged feathers and waits for them to grow back. After five months, the eagle is reborn and lives for another 30 years . . . pretty amazing.

When it rains, most birds head for shelter; the eagle is the only bird that, in order to avoid the rain, starts flying above the clouds. It can spot a rabbit moving almost a mile away. No wonder God wants us to spread our wings and soar with eagles. Sorry Ben, I'm glad you lost this one.

16

"Atheism: the belief that there was nothing and nothing happened to nothing, and then nothing magically exploded for no reason, creating everything; and then a bunch of everything magically rearranged itself, for no reason whatsoever, into self-replicating bits, which then turned into dinosaurs." Are we all clear now?

There was a young man , late teens, long ago who wanted to start his life's adventure and find his place in the world. Strong, handsome, intelligent are some of the descriptions used to describe him; he knew he wanted to do something . . . something important and meaningful. He had always been drawn to the allure of the ocean and ships, he thought it all sounded very exciting and rewarding. Now, these were the days before recruitment centers or any draft, or much of any formal signing centers. No, in these days you simply went down to the docks and located a ship's captain and told him you wanted to join the Navy.

They would check you out, give you a cursory physical, ask a few questions and take you on board.

After the young man had checked out the situation and preliminarily talked to the Navy people, he knew without doubt this was what he wanted to do. He was very excited and because of his stature and education and general bearing, he was even being offered a commission into officer's training. All beyond his wildest dreams. He quickly explained it all to his parents and family and friends and started making plans for his new career—-one he knew he was destined for.

The day finally came that he was to depart, he had his duffel bag packed, had tied up all his affairs, said all his goodbyes, now he and his mother made the short trip down to the docks for him to formally enlist and board the ship for his maiden voyage. He was very excited, in fact, he kept racing ahead of his mother as they walked, he could hardly wait to get there. As they arrived, the ship looked spectacular, the officers were dressed in their finest uniforms and the crew was busily preparing for departure.

As he walked up to the ship, the commanding officer greeted him and showed him to his quarters where he could store his duffel bag. After he had properly stored his bag he went back outside to say goodbye to his mother who was waiting on him. His mother looked deeply into his eyes for several moments, not uttering a single word. Finally the young man asked her if she was okay, she said "I don't think this is what the Lord has planned for you." Without another word, he turned away, went back onto the ship, into his quarters, retrieved his duffel bag, told the captain he had changed his mind , left the ship with his mother and went back home.

How many of today's young people would have done that? How many would have given up their dreams, listened to their mother and without question, changed their entire future? I think most young men, today and then, would have said " oh Mother, you worry too much, this is what I want to do and I'm going to do it." Not our man, not George Washington . . . he trusted his mother, trusted that she had insight into what the Lord had planned for him, and somehow must have known the Lord had a better plan for him, than he had for himself.

Would he have made a great sailor . . . Yes. Would he have made a great Admiral . . . undoubtedly yes. But oh, aren't we glad he listened to his mother that fateful day and decided not to join the BRITISH NAVY! Can you imagine our country fighting without George Washington? Even worse, can you imagine us fighting against him—I don't want to think about it. Truly, the Lord has a better plan for us than we do for ourselves; if only we would listen and trust and have faith.

17

"Don't take yourself so seriously. No one else does."

Some of you may remember the tennis champion Michael Chang, he played professionally in the late 80's and 90's. The odd thing about sports is that around 30-35 years old you're considered old. So , when we remember Michael Chang we think of him as being retired and old, but, he's not—he's still a young man , he just doesn't play professional tennis anymore. Michael was at various times ranked in the top five players in the world—which was a great accomplishment for him since most of his competitors were over 6' tall and Michael was "only" 5' 9." He was always battling stronger, taller players, however, his speed on the court, his consistency and his incredible mental toughness carried him to heights few thought he could obtain.

Probably his greatest tennis accomplishment was when he won the French Open at the age of 17; the first American to win on the slow red clay in Paris since Tony Trabert in the early 1950's. The French Open is a tough tournament to win—especially for Americans, since we don't have any of the notoriously slow clay to practice on. Most American players grew up on hard courts and like the consistency of the bounce and the speed of the court—the French has been brutal for Americans. Most of our greatest players have never won there: Jimmy Conners, John McEnroe and even the greatest of them all Pete Sampras went their entire careers without winning the French Open. So, how did Michael Chang do it? Beating two of the greatest players of all time in the semi finals and finals—Ivan Lendl and Stefan Edberg. I don't know . . . And I'm not sure Michael could tell you either; but even though he never won another Grand Slam tournament in his career—he won that one.

I'm pretty sure Michael knew he had help that day in Paris . . . During the awards ceremony he first and foremost thanked the Lord Jesus Christ for allowing him to play his best. Now, you and I both know the Lord doesn't care who wins a tennis match, or a ball game, or a race . . . I'm sure He has more important things on His agenda . . . Right?

Michael's parents came to the United States from China for a better opportunity and for a better future for their two sons, Michael and his older brother Carl. Michael's grandparents stayed in China but the family was very close and always kept in contact with each other and visited whenever possible. Unfortunately, Michael's grandmother developed a type of cancer when Michael was very young and even though the doctor's tried everything, nothing seemed to help. She did every therapy and treatment and drug known at the time and nothing could stop this horrible disease from consuming her. Finally, the doctor's told her there was nothing else they could do except try to make her comfortable for the remaining few months of her life.

A young missionary in her home town in China heard of her illness and stopped by one day to visit, she asked if it would be okay to pray to the Lord for His healing touch. Michael's grandmother obviously had nothing to lose at that point and told the woman it was okay, even though she knew nothing about this Jesus person. After the prayers were said, the woman left and Michael's grandmother fell off to sleep for the night. The next morning she didn't feel quite as sick as she did the day before—that was good news, finally a good day amongst all the bad ones. The next day she felt good as well, and during the weeks ahead, she felt better and better, even though all treatments and medicines had been stopped. . Her doctors brought her back in the hospital to try and figure out what was happening and could find no evidence of the cancer in her body.

They were dumbfounded, never had they seen anything so bad, so out of control, so terminal be completely healed. Michael's grandmother immediately converted to Christianity, as well as all her family, and lived many more years in good health afterwards. This was the reason Michael's family in America were Christians. Okay, but still, Jesus doesn't care who wins the French Open; sure, he can and does do miracles like with Michael's grandmother, but a sporting event is not in this classification . . . is it?

During the middle week of the French Open tennis tournament that year the Tiannemen Square people's revolt happened in Beijing, China. The Chinese government cracked down swiftly and hard, causing many Chinese to lose hope. Then, less than one week later a 17 year old Chinese American Christian, with no experience, no ranking, and given no chance, shocks the world by winning the French Open. Did this give the Chinese people something to be proud of, something to smile about, something to ease the burden of Tiannamen Square? Hopefully it did. And, maybe the Lord did care who won that tennis match.

18

"Don't measure yourself by what you have accomplished, but by what you should have accomplished with your ability."

John Wooden

Sometimes you gotta run. . . . run

Just leave it all behind and run

To a more familiar place

With a hundred smiling faces

And fall into the sweet embrace

Of home.

19

"The pursuit of happiness is the chief cause of unhappiness."

Why We Celebrate the 4th of July

Have you ever wondered what happened to the 56 men who signed the Declaration of Independence? For all intents and purposes, these men were signing their death warrants unless America won the war. If the British had won, they would have been hanged, or shot, for treason. Their bravery is sometimes forgotten today, but we should remember these gallant men who put their country and its ideals ahead of their own safety and lives. I would like to think there are some people in Washington today who have the same set of ideals and bravery these men had . . . I would like to think that.

Five signers were captured by the British as traitors, and tortured before they died.

Twelve had their homes ransacked and burned.

Two lost their sons serving in the Revolutionary Army; another had two sons captured.

Nine of the 56 fought and died from wounds or hardships of the Revolutionary War.

What kind of men were they?

24 were lawyers and jurists.

11 were merchants, 9 were farmers and large plantation owners; men of means, well educated, but they signed the Declaration of Independence knowing full well that the penalty would be death if they were captured.

Carter Braxton of Virginia, a wealthy planter and trader, saw his own ships swept from the seas by the British Navy. He sold his home and properties to pay his debts, and died in rags.

Thomas McKeam was so hounded by the British that he was forced to move his family almost constantly. He served in the Congress without pay, and his family was kept in hiding. His possessions were taken from him, and poverty was his reward.

Vandals or soldiers looted the properties of Dillery, Hall, Clymer, Walton, Gwinnett, Heyward, Ruttledge and Middleton.

At the battle of Yorktown, the British General Cornwallis had taken over the home of Thomas Nelson, Jr. for his headquarters. Mr. Nelson quietly urged General George Washington to open fire on his house, destroying it. He died bankrupt.

Francis Lewis had his home and properties destroyed. The enemy jailed his wife, and she died within a few months.

John Hart was driven from his wife's bedside as she was dying. Their 13 children fled for their lives. His fields and gristmill were laid to waste. For more than a year he lived in forests and caves, returning home to find his wife dead and his children vanished.

So, take a few minutes to think about what the 4th of July means to us now and what these brave men had to endure to ensure our freedom . . . freedom, by the way, which is never free.

20

"Truth is, everybody is going to hurt you; you just have to find the ones worth suffering for."

Bob Marley

Okay, back to my friends . . . Dickie; not just my friend, he's everybody's friend. He's one guy who a dozen people consider their best friend . . . he's that kind of man. We've been very close for over 50 years—-I know him and he knows me; there's very few secrets. In fact, he knows more about me than I do; seemingly the years have diminished my memories somewhat, or they have enhanced his memories because every time we see each other he's telling me stories of things I have absolutely no recollection of. I remember him cooking us bacon sandwiches before ball games, and camping out and walking around town at midnight, and making scuffing noises on the floor with his shoes and blaming the sound on Sylvia McArthur, and riding around town in his car that had a 45 rpm record player in it . . . yes, it truly did.

And I remember some of the Vardell Hall stories, others are a little foggy and left to interpretation. Whether these stories are actually true or not is really of no consequence . . . the fun is listening to him tell them!

Where to start? I've been playing ball with Dickie and against him as long as I can remember. Mrs. Warren (my all-time favorite teacher, Mrs. Hudgins being a close second) always chose me and Dickie to pick teams during recess in the sixth grade—she wouldn't let us be on the same team. The first time I ever played basketball with black guys was at Dickie's house; we played with a guy named GG (for Green Giant). And he was a giant to us; probably 6'6" and could run and jump, we were duly impressed. Needless to say, GG against some 5'7" skinny white boys was not much of a challenge—-but it was great fun. We also played some sandlot baseball against a guy known as "Sloppy Joe" who hit balls OVER the cotton gin, left handed and right handed! We couldn't even hit the cotton gin with a fungo from second base—and Sloppy Joe hit it over . . . wow.

Being the sports nuts that we were and also being short and skinny like we were, we had to improvise. Case in point, we wanted to dunk; obviously we couldn't, so Dickie got a second rim and nailed it to tree about 8 ½ ' up (instead of 10) so we could dunk—and boy did we ever! We could do everything Billy Cunningham did . . . sort of. Dickie lived about 3-4 blocks from me so I was at his house a lot; great memories of me and him pitching to his Dad in the yard. His Dad would always Oooh and Aaah at our so-called curve balls (which MAYBE broke a couple of inches), but his Dad made you feel like Whitey Ford out there.

A great memory I have is of me and Dickie together scoring 25 points in the first half of a high school basketball game . . . it was truly amazing; I didn't miss a shot and he didn't miss many. I think our total of my 2 points and his 23 points still stands as a first half record for the Red Devils. Those were such fun days, I wish I could remember them better; however, my friend remembers them all: who scored what and who dated who. He even remembers a baseball game when we were freshman who didn't get to play at all, we had a lot of juniors and seniors on that team, so us four freshman (Dickie, Michael Davis, Norman Furmage and me) mostly sat on the bench. End of the year we're playing some team and beating them pretty bad, so our coach decides to let Dickie pinch hit—-now, remember, he hasn't batted all season long. Dickie gets up to the plate, looks over to the coach in the 3rd base coaching box and the coach gives him the bunt sign. The bunt sign! He hasn't hit all year and coach wants him to bunt—well, old Dickie took three mighty swings and struck out; but by Gosh he didn't bunt; nor did he bat again that year.

After high school my good buddy joined the Army with our friend Jerry and was eventually stationed in Korea for 13 months, whereby he made new friends and even brought one home with him, John Pollock, and turned him into a Red Devil . . . for a few years anyway. Then, my friend gets married and has a son and finds his true calling in life—being a Dad, and a darned good one at that. For whatever reasons, his marriage didn't last and Dickie ended up with custody of his son Brent. He became the kind of dad we'd all aspire to be, if we could. Coached his little league teams, played catch with him in the yard, took him to ball games, took him to movies, took him to visit me and my little snaggle-toothed daughter. He didn't just spend "quality time" with Brent; he spent "quantity time" with Brent—which is altogether more important. I admired him for sacrificing his life—to an extent—to make sure Brent's life was fulfilling and rewarding—which it truly was. Brent turned out to be a very successful, college graduate and professional businessman, as well as a devoted husband and father as well. A true consequence of being raised by a good man.

There were years when Dickie, and the rest of us, did some crazy things; those stories are private and only told amongst ourselves . . . they would bore the rest of you anyway. How do you describe a man who has probably been to more ballgames than anyone in North Carolina? Spends vacations going to Major League and minor league ballparks? Keeps up with untold high school acquaintances, is a Deacon in the church, sings in the choir and still has time to visit with me and tell and re-tell the stories of our youth that we so love to hear? How do you describe him?

He's my friend, that's how. A great and good man that I'm very proud of.

Dickie

21

"If you're lucky enough to be Irish, then you're lucky enough."

Remember the old game show from the 1950's and 60's, "What's my Line? Probably not, unless you're old like me. But, let's play . . . I'll give you hints and you tell me what this profession is:

> You must be between 5'10" and 6'2," with a waist size that cannot exceed 30"

> You must commit 2 years of your life to this profession

> You must live on the job

> You cannot drink alcohol on or off duty FOR THE REST OF YOUR LIFE.

> You cannot swear in public FOR THE REST OF YOUR LIFE, nor disgrace your profession in any way.

After your two years, you're given a wreath pin that is worn to signify your duty. There are only 400 presently worn.

You must obey all these rules for the rest of your life, or give up your pin.

> Who am I? The guard at the tomb of the Unknown Soldier at Arlington National Cemetary.

The first six months of duty a guard cannot talk to anyone, nor watch television. All off duty time is spent studying the 175 notable people laid to rest in the cemetery. A guard memorizes who they are and where they are interred.

Every guard spends five hours a day getting his uniforms ready for guard duty.

In 2003 as Hurricane Isabelle was approaching Washington, DC, the US Senate and House took 2 days off with anticipation of the storm. Because of the dangers of the approaching storm the members assigned the duty of guarding the Tomb of the Unknown Soldier were given permission to suspend the assignment. They respectfully declined the offer, "No way, Sir!" Soaked to the skin, marching in the pelting rain of a tropical storm, they said that guarding the Tomb was not just an assignment, it was the highest honor that can be afforded to a serviceperson. The tomb has been patrolled continuously , 24/7, since 1930.

22

"Everybody dies, but not everybody lives."

First, eggs were bad for you, then they are okay, now they may be bad again; then red meat was very bad for you, now it's sort of okay; I'm pretty sure smoking is still bad for you. But . . . what about coffee? I've heard it all about the effects and causes of too much coffee, or not enough coffee. I personally love a cup in the morning, addicted might be a better word—whether it's good or bad, I'm going to drink a cup in the morning. Most people are this way I think, except for my friend Jerry who refuses to succumb to coffee's allure—he's stronger than me.

I found an interesting article endorsed by the American Heart Association and the Harvard School of Public Health . . . I don't think they'd intentionally lie to us; here's what they say about coffee:

Coffee contains antioxidants, vitamins and minerals and a few dietary proteins.

Research shows coffee consumption has reduced the risk of some diseases and ailments, including:

>Parkinson's
>
>Alzheimer's
>
>Type 2 diabetes
>
>Gallstones
>
>Cancer–oral, esophageal and pharyngeal
>
>Asthma attacks
>
>Heart rhythm problems
>
>Strokes
>
>Cirrhosis of the liver
>
>Caffeine increases the effectiveness of certain types of painkillers ; acting as a stimulant

Women who drank 5 cups a day were 57% less likely to have estrogen receptor-negative concerns than those who drank less than a cup a day. And, heavy coffee drinkers had 20% less risks of contracting any kind of breast cancer when age was taken into account.

Men who drank at least 6 cups a day were 60% less likely than non-coffee drinkers to develop the most lethal forms of prostate cancer. They were 20% less likely to develop any form of the disease. Men who drank 1-3 cups per day were 30% less likely to develop the deadliest form of prostate cancer.

But , hold on Jerry, before I convert you, there are some negative results from overconsumption as well.

    Negative effects may include:

        Changes in sleep pattern

        May cause auditory hallucinations

        Hampers absorption of some minerals and vitamins, such as magnesium, zinc and iron

        Can raise blood pressure

        Mild diuretic could lead to dehydration and a loss of Vitamin B and C

        Can stain your teeth

        Acids can aggravate heartburn

So, after digesting this information, it is indeed up to us each to decide how we fell about coffee. However you feel, take heed . . . I'm sure in a few months another study will come out and we'll to reevaluate the whole mess again. In the meantime, I'll have a double espresso please.

23

"I'm an old man and have known a great many troubles, but most of them never happened."

Mark Twain

More weird facts

Rats multiply so quickly that in 18 months, two rats could have over a million descendants.

Only 2% of Caribbean islands are inhabited.

If the government has no knowledge of aliens, then why does Title 14, Section 1211 of the Code of Federal Regulations , implemented on July 16, 1969, make it illegal for U.S. citizens to have any contact with extraterrestrials or their vehicles?

A duck's quack doesn't echo, and no one knows why.

23% of all photocopier faults world-wide are caused by people sitting on them and photocopying their butts.

Most lipstick contains fish scales.

In a study of 200,000 ostriches over a period of 80 years, no one reported a single case where an ostrich buried it's head in the sand.

It is physically impossible for pigs to look up into the sky.

More than 50% of the people in the world have never made or received a telephone call.

On average, 100 people choke to death on ballpoint pens every year.

Again, on average, people fear spiders more than they do death.

90% of New York City cabbies are recently arrived immigrants.

Only one person in two billion will live to be 116 or older.

Women blink nearly twice as much as men do.

A snail can sleep for three years.

The electric chair was invented by a dentist.

Americans, on average, eat 18 acres of pizza every day.

More than 100,000,000 trees worth of junk mail arrives in U.S. mailboxes each year.

Finally,

Tobacco is a $200 billion industry, producing six trillion cigarettes a year—-about 1,000 cigarettes for each person on earth. And this is what you'll find in cigarettes:

> Formaldehyde, which embalmers use to preserve dead bodies;
>
> Toluene, which is commonly used as an ingredient in paint thinner;
>
> Acetone, an active ingredient in nail polish remover;
>
> Ammonia, which lets you absorb more nicotine, keeping you hooked on smoking.

If you smoke, you and those around you are inhaling arsenic, benzene, cadmium, hydrogen cyanide, lead, mercury and phonol. In all, 400 harmful chemicals, including 44 types of poison, of which 43 are proven cancer-causing substances.

And yet . . .

24

"Nobody can go back and start a new beginning, but anyone can start today and make a new ending."

Tough question number 1:

If you knew a woman who was pregnant, who had 8 kids already, three who were deaf, two who were blind, one mentally retarded, and she had syphilis . . . would you recommend that she have an abortion?

If you said YES, you just killed Beethoven.

Tough question number 2

It's time to elect a new world leader and ONLY your vote counts. Here are the facts about the three candidates. Who would you vote for?

Candidate A

Associates with crooked politicians, and consults with astrologist. He's had two mistresses. He also chain smokes and drinks 8 to 10 martinis a day.

Candidate B

He was kicked out of office twice, sleeps until noon, used opium in college and drinks a quart of whiskey every evening.

Candidate C

He is a decorated war hero. He's a vegetarian, doesn't smoke, drinks an occasional beer and never cheated on his wife.

Candidate A is Franklin D. Roosevelt

Candidate B is Winston Churchill

Candidate C is Adolph Hitler

Makes a person think before judging someone doesn't it?

25

"Things turn out best for the people who make the best of the way things turn out."

John Wooden

And now, my friend Jerry; like the other guys, a great and good man . . . I wish I was more like him (though not entirely, he can be a bit OCD at times). He and I have a sort of bond, in that neither of us grew up with a father in our homes . . . however, I don't think we missed it all that much either. We're both fairly normal, Jerry more than me, and he can throw the best bounce pass I've ever seen.

We were in each other's first weddings way back when, and for various reasons, we were both divorced after several years. Then we both married school teachers—pretty ones at that—and have kept these two cute, little girls with us for quite a while now. Jerry's wife, Wandre, was (and is), perfect for him—keeps him straight. I could take a few paragraphs to explain how great a dad he's been to Scott, Emily and Ryan . . . but I couldn't do it adequately—not even close. I could tell you how great a husband and son-in-law he's been, but there's not enough time. I could tell you all he does for his church and the Frozen Chosen, words aren't descriptive enough. Jerry . . . he's beyond description.

My wife and I have travelled some with Jerry and Wandre and visited them often over the years—always a joy. We drove up the coast highway from Los Angeles to San Francisco and back one time, the memories of that trip are so pure, it's like a dream now. We've been on a cruise, we've been to Jamaica, the Grove Park Inn, various Bed & Breakfasts, the beach—we know them well. We've been through the sadness of losing our mothers and the various trials and tribulations children will put you through. But, through it all, old Jer is constant . . . a rock who can be counted on for comfort and strength.

Exactly how we became such good friends is a little perplexing to me when I think of it; he didn't go to the First Baptist Church like the rest of us—he grew up in a different section of town. He doesn't particularly like baseball and never played it (which I don't understand to this day how a human being cannot like baseball). He didn't pursue the Vardell Hall girls like me and Dickie and D.L. and Furman and most Red Springs boys—weren't we the lucky ones to have a private girl's school in our little town of 4,000 people. But the boy loved to play basketball, if we could get him out of bed to play that is. Can't tell you how many times we'd go to Jerry's house to get him to play and he'd still be in bed . . . 11:00 or 12:00, he's still sleeping! Remember, this was in the days of 3 stations on your television . . . They played the national anthem and signed off around midnight—there was nothing else to watch. So, why did he stay up so late and sleep all morning? Only he can answer that, but don't ask him because he might answer.

While the rest of played baseball, Jerry ran, and ran, and ran . . . and ran. The boy could run all day and night, he has this big chest that holds over-sized lungs is all I can figure. We'd be sitting in school , daydreaming, thinking about Mary Nelson, or Tana, or Barbara or Wanda or Pam or Dianne (you get the picture) , and during lunch or PE class, we'd see Jerry running around the track. Running, running, running—you'd get dizzy looking at him, but he just kept on running. I'm certain he could've parlayed that into a college scholarship if he'd tried, he was down in the low 4 minutes for a mile run—which was impressive. But the boy loved basketball . . . just loved it. He eventually ended up at a small college where he made the basketball team and during one memorable game actually blocked a shot taken by a 7 foot future NBA star—Artis Gilmore; yep, my buddy blocked a shot by a future NBA star . . . I am still impressed to this very day!

Army, college, kids, marriage, divorce, remarriage, nice jobs, etc., through it all, he's always been a man you can count on, a man you can trust, a man you'd love to be your friend. That's where I'm the lucky one . . . he's my friend.

Jerry

26

In grade school John Lennon was asked what he wanted to be when he grew up--he said "HAPPY," the teacher said, "you don't understand the question." John said, "you don't understand me."

For anyone to have five close friends for over 50 years is a remarkable thing; in my opinion, I've truly been blessed. These five guys and I have been through a lot, seen a lot and done a lot . . . Some of it we can even talk about in public, some of it we've forgotten; but we always have Dickie to re-tell those old stories and even make up new endings when appropriate. As for me, my luck continues to grow; I've added a new best friend to this group of five. Though I've only know him for about 5 years, I can assure you, he's a good, old boy. Mark grew up somewhere up in the Midwestern northlands, some remote outpost of cold winters and even colder summers . . . that might not be true—but , it might.

I'm just glad Marky migrated to a less extreme locale, met my little sister and married her . . . whew! What a relief that was. I call him Marky for a reason, and right or wrong, I'm sticking to my reason, perhaps it's superstition, but I'm not taking any chances. My little sister had a succession of failed suitors in her life, they could not measure up to her high standards and in one case . . . well, I won't go there. The point being, all of these lotharios had ONE SYLLABLE names: Tim, Nick, Pat, Ray, etc., etc. etc. Now knowing how perfect my sister is, I'm positive it must be these crazy one-syllable name dudes. Makes sense right? Look at my friends: Jer-ry, Dick-ie, Al-len, Lar-ry, me—Gar-y, my daughter, Shel-ley, Kal-I, my neice, Cas-ey, my wife, Sus-an . . . so there was no way we were going to jinx this romance with a one syllable name . . . .he knew going in and going forward till death do us part . . . he's Mark-y.

Marky's good traits: he's a great Dad to his two sons and a great Dad to Anne's daughter as well; he's a great and loving son and an excellent husband. His next good trait: he loves baseball; secondary traits: he loves basketball, football, golf, hurling and Irish football—not necessarily in that order. On a recent trip to The Emerald Isle, the other four of us were exploring and shopping; somehow Marky got separated from us, but we weren't too concerned, it was a small, little village in Ireland and I had the keys to the car. We found him later, holed up in a little pub, Guinness in hand thoroughly engrossed in a hurling match between County Clare (fairest of them all) and County Kerry (my homeland). He didn't quite understand the rules of hurling, but was cheering them on like the good, old boy he is.

He treats my sister well, maybe too well; case in point: my sister called me one night to check in and there was a lot of background noise where she was calling from. I said "where are you?" "At the indoor tennis courts" she said, "I'm hitting hundreds of balls with the automatic tennis machine." Wow, I said, what's Marky doing while you're hitting all those tennis balls? Did you leave him home or something? "No," she said, "he's here picking up all the balls for me." He's a good, old boy—and my sister is spoiled!

Mark and Anne

27

"It's never too late to be what you might have been."

The final friend I'm going to write about, I've known for 23 years, and trust me, he's one of a kind. He's my wife's Dad, Conrad Carter. He is 92 years old, vigorous, healthy, Godly, wise and extremely intelligent. He knows more about the Bible than any preacher I know, except for Billy Graham probably. At 92, he gets up and does some form of exercising each day (pay attention everyone), has a morning devotional with his beautiful wife Barbara, checks his emails for all things Republican, then plays the rest of the day in the stock market—and, he's a GOOD player.

I know first hand that he's been a great dad because he has two beautiful, intelligent , Godly daughters to prove that; one of them might have a "little" temper and the other might be a "little" . . . well, those of you who know Martha can fill in the blank here. But, they were raised right; Conrad and his first wife, also Barbara, did an excellent job of insuring that. Recently, my wife Susan and I had the pleasure of visiting with Conrad and Barbara and going out to lunch as well; as lunch was over , Susan and Barbara were walking ahead of us and Conrad grabbed my arm and said "How is Susan really doing?" After 60 years, he's still concerned about his little girl . . . I said, "she's fine, she's doing great." He then said, "sometimes I worry about that girl." I guess a Dad never stops worrying about his girls; but he shouldn't . . . He and his wife did an outstanding job of being role models and parents. As with my other friends . . . .he's truly a great and wonderful man.

Barbara, Conrad, and Susan

28

"For the truly faithful, no miracle is necessary; for those who doubt, no miracle is sufficient."

There are places I'll remember

All my life, though some have changed

Some forever, not for better

Some have gone and some remain

All these places have their moments

With lovers and friends, I still can recall

Some are dead and some are living

In my life, I've loved them all.

But of all these friends and lovers

There is no one compares with you

And these memories lose their meaning

When I think of love as something new

Though I know I'll never lose affection

For people and things that went before

I know I'll often stop and think about them

In my life, I love you more.

John

29

"Time you enjoy wasting, is not wasted."

J. Lennon

I live in Winston-Salem, a nice, comfortable city of fine universities, a school of the arts, industry, sports, history, business, research . . . generally, just a cool place to live; and, with a variety of wildlife within the city limits. And within my house. I've had a bat flying in my house—thought I would never get it to fly out the open door; a snake, which was very creepy; and an owl, which perched on the mantel piece staring at us. Like many others , I was bothered by raccoons getting in my garbage cans , so I borrowed a trap from the city's wildlife department and set it out with a piece of bread covered with peanut butter as bait. The first night I caught a cat; the second night I caught a possum (who really played possum—it fooled me, I thought it was dead); the third night I caught the same, stupid cat again. Then, I caught 2 squirrels and another possum–maybe, the same one, I'm not sure, they tend to all look alike to me—furry and ugly.

Finally, after nearly a week I caught a mean, hissing, spitting snarling raccoon. What a scary animal it was, I'm sure if it could've gotten out of the cage, it would have attacked me for sure. Then I caught more raccoons four out of the next five nights . . . I finally tired of this ordeal; catching them, driving them out in the country and releasing them without getting attacked and bitten. So, I turned in my cage and we have a truce with the raccoon population now.

I saw a fox one morning next to my trash can . . . it stood completely still watching me watching him, for about 90 seconds or so; then it trotted away while looking over his shoulder to make sure I wasn't following him. That was very cool, but the coyote in my front yard was even better. It was just loping along, not in any hurry, nor concerned who was looking at it him or following him—which I tried to do for a couple of blocks before it cut through a yard and disappeared into the woods. I regularly see deer tracks all over our yard and see them, usually at sunrise , throughout our neighborhood.

If you're vigilant, it's also common to spot red-tailed hawks and sharp-shinned hawks in the trees in my yard . . . very impressive animals. I would imagine the abundance of squirrels, chipmunks, the occasional groundhog and songbirds in my yard make for a good hunting ground. All are welcome . . . except the snakes; just too creepy and scary for me. I've only seen the coyote once, but he's welcome back anytime, it won't have any problems from me.

There are also wild turkeys around our neighborhood, though I haven't seen any in my yard, I do see them close by, as well as the majestic soaring vultures and blue herons. I saw a television special about wild turkeys that was fascinating . . . Newly born wild turkeys would find non-poisonous snakes in the woods and pick them up, throw them, peck at them, seemingly just play with them; but they would go nowhere near poisonous snakes. How did they know which was which? This was a group of new born turkeys whose mother was killed and they were raised by a human. They were obviously born knowing which snake was dangerous and which was not. What other senses are animals born with we don't understand? So many questions that we'll never fully comprehend, only marvel at God's creations. Large and small, they are all truly amazing to see (as long as they stay out of my house).

I've been fortunate to observe, in the wild, flocks of 40-50 bald eagles all together on a fishing pier at a cove in Ketchikan, Alaska; I saw an osprey dive into the Yellowstone River and come up with a fish, only to see an eagle dive at the osprey and steal the fish from it in midair. I was on a raft trip on the Snake River with my daughter and we were chased down the river for about 50 yards by a bull moose when we came too close to him as he was feeding on a small island in the river—that was a tad scary I must add. Our hiking party of 4 was tracked by a mountain lion in Utah for at least a mile or so; we ran into a dead end and doubled back only to see the mountain lion tracks on top of our previous footprints—however, we never actually saw the lion itself. I've seen grizzly bears in Montana and other states as well. We woke up one morning to see several elk sleeping in front of our cottage in Banff, Canada; on the same trip, mountain goats came up to us and ate cookies from our hands—I know we shouldn't do that, it was my sister's idea, not mine. We had another elk come to our stopped car and stick it's head in our window looking for food I presume, it slobbered all over the seat.

In Alaska, I've been on a small boat in the bay within a hundred yards of several whales—an extremely awesome sight, not scary at all, just awe inspiring. I was driving through Wyoming once and a herd of wild horses were running parallel to the road and I slowed to their speed and "rode" with them for about 45 seconds—there was no fencing on that range; must have been 10-15 horses just running with the wind, free and wild, as they were meant to be. We got too close to a herd of buffalo in Yellowstone, they are massive animals , they scared my daughter so bad that she jumped into the car and wet her pants—-and I don't blame her!

These and many other experiences with nature are what make our memories; even the most simple things like a Canadian Jay landing on my foot when I was sitting down on top of a mountain in Jasper National Park, can be a memory that lasts forever. So many other stories, so many memories . . . thank you Lord for the varied and incredible animals we share this great, big, beautiful world with.

30

"All that is necessary for evil to succeed is that good men do nothing."

In the past years the United States has provided direct cash aid to :

Haiti $1.4 billion

Iraq   1.08 billion

Libya   1.45 billion

Pakistan   2 billion

Congo   359 million

Egypt   397 million

Ethiopia   981 million

Hamas   351 million

Jordon   463 million

Kenya	816 million
Kazakhstan	304 million
Mexico	622 million
Mozambique	404 million
Nigeria	456 million
Russia	380 million
Senegal	698 million
South Africa	566 million
Sudan	870 million
Tanzania	554 million
Uganda	451 million
Zambia	331 million

And yet, most (if not all) of these countries HATE us! How many came to our aid on 9/11?

Should we not help those who can't help themselves? Should we not help provide for those who receive no aid at all? Should we not help the homeless? The orphans? The elderly? The mentally ill?

Should we not start in America first?

3/

"A patriot must always be ready to defend his country against his government."

Edward Abbey

One country we don't give money to is Israel; that tiny, little country surrounded by the Muslim world. . . . God's chosen people, who most world citizens tend to denigrate. Let's examine some facts about this little country and its people:

The Middle East has been growing date palms for centuries. The average tree is about 18-20 feet tall and yields about 38 pounds of dates a year.

Israeli date trees are now yielding 400 pounds/year and are short enough to be harvested from the ground or a short ladder .

Israel the 100th smallest country, with less than 1/1000th of the world's population, can lay claim to the following:

The cell phone was developed in Israel by Israelis working in the Israeli branch of Motorola, which has its largest development center in Israel.

The Pentium microprocessor in your computer was most likely made in Israel.

Voice mail technology was developed in Israel.

Both Microsoft and Cisco built their only R&D facilities outside the US in Israel.

The technology for the AOL Instant Messenger ICQ was developed in 1996 by four young Israelis.

Israel has the fourth largest air force in the world (after the U.S, Russia and China). In addition to a large variety of other aircraft, Israel's air force has an aerial arsenal of over 250 F-16's. This is the largest fleet of F-16 aircraft outside of the U. S.

Israel has the highest percentage in the world of home computers per capita.

According to industry officials, Israel designed the airline industry's most impenetrable flight security. US officials now look (finally) to Israel for advice on how to handle airborne security threats.

Israel has the highest ratio of university degrees to the population in the world.

Israel produces more scientific papers per capita than any other nation by a large margin—109 per 10,000 people—as well as one of the highest per capita rates of patents filed.

With more than 3,000 high-tech companies and startups, Israel has the highest concentration of hi-tech companies in the world—apart from the Silicon Valley, U.S.

On a per capita basis, Israel has the largest number of biotech startups.

Twenty-four per cent of Israel's workforce holds university degrees, ranking third in the industrialized world, after the United States and Holland and 12 per cent hold advanced degrees.

Israel has the third highest rate of entrepreneurship—and the highest rate among women and among people over 55—in the world.

Israel is the only country in the world that entered the 21st century with a net gain in its number of trees, made more remarkable because this was achieved in an area considered mainly desert.

Israel has more museums per capita than any other country.

An Israeli company developed a computerized system for ensuring proper administration of medications, thus removing human error from medical treatment. Every year in U. S. hospitals 7,000 patients die from treatment mistakes.

Israel's Given Imaging developed the first ingestible video camera, so small it fits inside a pill. Used to view the small intestine from the inside, cancer and digestive disorders.

Israel leads the world in the number of scientists and technicians in the workforce, with 145 per 10,000, as opposed to 85 in the U. S., over 70 in Japan, and less than 60 in Germany. With over 25% of its work force employed in technical professions. Israel places first in this category as well.

An Israeli company was the first to develop and install a large-scale solar-powered and fully functional electricity generating plant, in southern California's Mojave desert.

All the above while engaged in regular wars with an implacable enemy that seeks its destruction, and an economy continuously under strain by having to spend more per capita on its own protection than any other county on earth.

Our country was founded on Christian values; like it or not, it's the truth. Read our Declaration of Independence, our Constitution, virtually any documents our founding fathers penned—they all reference our dependence on God. Recently, our government has been trying to eliminate God from our country; it wants to take Him out of our schools, out of our courts, out of our businesses . . . out of EVERYTHING!

Before the government started this elimination process, the U.S. was 1st in industrialized nations in school test scores in 17 different categories—-EVERY ONE. Since taking God out of our schools, we are last, or next to last, in each and every one.

Israel is God's chosen land, but WE are blessed by God, from sea to shining sea. However, if we keep telling God we don't want Him in our schools, our government, our homes, our businesses . . . well, soon enough He'll listen to us and give us what we want and I don't think we're going to like it. Let us please take Israel's example, and our Founding Father's advice . . . Keep God in our lives, trust Him to lead us; I guarantee you He has a better plan for our country than the so-called politicians do who are leading us now.

32

"Pain is temporary, it may last 1 minute, 1 hour, 1 week, or 1 year... but if you quit-that lasts forever."

QUESTIONS

From Nick: "Am I going to heaven when I die?"

If you believe in Jesus and repent of your sins and trust in him... YES. There is no other way. You've heard from the media and talk shows that there are many roads and paths to Heaven; and they are correct in that all roads do indeed lead to heaven, when we die we will all come face to face with the Lord to give an account of our lives; those who believed in the Lord Jesus will ENTER heaven. Those who rejected Him will not. There is nothing you can do on earth to "get into heaven" short of believing in the Lord. It doesn't matter how many so-called good deeds you do, how much good work you do, how good a person you are, how kind you are, how much you have sacrificed... the ONLY thing that matters is did you accept Jesus as your Lord and savior and repent of your sins.

Jesus said, "I am the resurrection and the life. He who believes in Me, though he may die, he shall live. And whoever lives and believes in Me shall never die." Unbelief and rejection break God's heart because He knows the consequences. When the human heart is shut and rejects Him, He will not force His way in; He will keep knocking and knocking and knocking . . . but He gave you the free will to choose and when we choose the wrong thing, He knows the ramifications here and in the life hereafter, and it breaks His heart. He does not want anyone to be destroyed, but to repent.

33

"As hard as a secret is to uncover, it's even harder to keep."

Also from Nick: "Do I still have time to atone for my sins?"

Remember when Jesus was being crucified with the two other men? One of them asked Jesus to forgive him there on the cross, just before he was going to die; Jesus did and told him, "Today, you will be with Me in paradise." So, yes, there is always time if you make the decision to accept Him. The problem some people have is they think they'll always have time, that they can live however they want to, do whatever they want, continue to live in sin and darkness and then, towards the end of their lives, just ask Jesus for forgiveness and everything will be fine.

The problem is, we don't know when we're going to die. The time of our death, as the time of births, is appointed by God, and we don't know when that will be. I'm sure the people in the World Trade Center on 9/11/01 didn't think they were going to die that fateful morning. Certainly, my cousin Joe didn't know he was going to die that day he was driving down the highway, just as you and I don't know when the Lord will take us from our earthly homes. We need to prepare and be ready . . . after all, this life is just dress rehearsal for the life we will live in infinity with the Lord.

From Bill: "Why is there so much suffering in the world?"

Our suffering does not escape God's notice; He is infinitely aware of everything going on in our world. How then, we might ask, can He allow such suffering to occur? God allows hardships in our lives so that our beliefs will become more real and our faith more substantial. Through hardships and trials we can exercise our faith and our trust in Him.

Anyone can be happy when they're peaceful and content, they're in great health and their world is at peace, but when storms come into our lives, that is the great test of our faith. It should be a powerful testimony to others when a believer can actually praise God while suffering. Maybe, just maybe, your suffering will be the vehicle to bring an unbeliever to God. People are watching us Christians, if you're in the midst of a troubling time, they're watching you to see how you react, that you'll practice what you preach. The way you handle suffering can bring great glory to God and maybe save a lost soul by your example. Remember the great Apostle Paul who was suffering from an unnamed "thorn in the flesh," he prayed and prayed for the Lord to relieve him from his suffering. The Lord replied "My grace is sufficient for you." And Paul set a great example for his followers . . . so God can be glorified through your suffering.

Sometimes, God can do things through our pain that couldn't be accomplished any other way. When our faith is tested, our endurance has a chance to grow; sometimes the Lord will turn a weakness into a strength. God may allow hardship into your life to make you stronger in your faith. Jesus made it abundantly clear that storms will come into every life. And when the storms come, it will become evident what kind of foundation we built our lives on.

God's goal is not to make us "happy," it's to make us "holy." It means having our faith intact when the sun is shining and the sky is blue as well as when the storm is raging and the journey is difficult. We must realize that God is in control of all circumstances surrounding our lives; the good and the so-called bad. He works them all "together for the good of those who love God and are called according to his purpose for them."

Remember, God told us . . ."For your present troubles are small and won't last very long. Yet they produce for us a glory that vastly outweighs them and will last forever." Some of the greatest lessons we learn in life come from our adversities; it gives us a compassion for others going through the same things. Real faith gets stronger through hardship, not weaker, it becomes more resilient. So press on when you're facing adversity and remember that God is there with you and that He is in control.

34

"When God tells us "NO," He means "NO, don't hurt yourselves."

From Frank: "Why did I get cancer?"

Being a Christian is not a guarantee that we will be exempt from suffering and disease. Christians will suffer, Christians will get cancer, Christians will have heart attacks and die while driving down the highway, Christians will die in automobile accidents and plane crashes. We face the same tragedies as everyone else.

Why did my friend Frank get cancer? I don't know. But I do know that God works all things together for good. I know He's in control and I know that He is good. And I know that I'll see my friend Frank in heaven one day and we'll have an infinity together with our cancer free, glorified, healthy , heavenly bodies.

35

"All journeys have secret destinations of which the traveler is unaware."

From Frank: "What is heaven like?"

Heaven is not simply a destination, and we need to stop thinking of it in a mystical way. The Bible describes heaven as an actual place, not a state of mind. The instant we die, we are in heaven the next instant; there is no holding pattern or various levels; as the Bible tells us, in the flash of an eye we are there. Jesus said, "I am going to prepare a "place" for you." Not a state of mind, or a mystical realm, but an actual place. The Bible describes heaven as a "city with eternal foundations, a city designed and built by God." Cities are places, they have buildings, homes, and art and music . . . this is what the Bible promises.

Heaven is also described in the Bible as a country or homeland; the Apostle Paul describes it as "paradise" . . . it's an actual place where we are going to receive our new heavenly bodies . . . the blueprints of our glorified bodies are in the bodies we now possess. Heaven will be joyful, our friends and relatives will be there (if they received Christ) and we'll have no more misery and sickness and sorrow. Will we know each other in heaven? Why would we know less in heaven than we do here?

Billy Graham was on "The Tonight Show" with Johnny Carson and Johnny asked the great evangelist this question: "Will there be golf in heaven?" Billy said, "Johnny, IF you get to heaven and golf is needed for your happiness and contentment . . . there will be golf in heaven."

36

"Not everything is good, but then again, Everything is."

From Wandre: "Could there have been another way for us to be saved rather than the torture Christ endured?"

The cross demonstrates the justice of God. And the justice of God requires that our sins be paid. He could not accept us into fellowship with Himself unless the penalty for sin was paid. Jesus had to endure the pain of the cross because humanity is sinful and there was no other way to bridge the gap between a just and holy God and sinful humanity.

The cross was Jesus' goal and it was His destination from the very beginning. He spoke of it frequently; so don't think the cross was a mistake, don't think the Romans or Jews or anyone else made him go to the cross . . . No. That was His intention from the beginning and He went there willingly to pay a price He didn't owe, so we could be one with God.

All other religions in the world say, "Do this, and you will find peace of mind . . ." "Do that and maybe you'll get to heaven." But it was done for us at the cross, paid for, completed, Jesus died there and rose again for us. At the cross, the righteous demands of God were satisfied; at the cross, our salvation was purchased.

37

"For God so loved the world, that He gave His only son, that whoever believes in Him, shall not perish, but have everlasting life."

From Nick: "What did you put me on earth for? (my purpose)"

In a nutshell, life is a preparation for eternity. We were not made to last forever, and God wants us to be with Him in heaven. One day we all will die and that will be the end of our earthly bodies, but not the end of us. We will live trillions of years in eternity, our life here on earth is the warm-up act, or dress rehearsal. God wants us to practice on earth what we will do forever in eternity.

Our life here on earth is a series of problems: either you're in one now, you're just coming out of one, or you're getting ready to go into on . . . but it's going to happen. The reason for this is that God is more interested in your character than your comfort. God is more interested in making your life holy than He is in making your life happy. We can be reasonably happy here on earth, but that's not the goal of life. The goal is to grow in character, in Christ likeness.

No matter how good things are in your life, there is always something bad that needs to be worked on. And no matter how bad things are in your life, there is always something good you can thank God for. You have to learn to deal with both the good and the bad of life. We need to ask ourselves: Am I going to live for possessions? Popularity? Am I going to be driven by pressures? Guilt? Bitterness? Materialism? Or , am I going to be driven by God's purposes for my life?

God didn't put you on earth just to fulfill a to-do list. He's more interested in what I am than what I do. We were put on this earth to know and love God–nothing else will satisfy us. That's why so many people are lonely and unhappy because they haven't found God. He made us with a longing in our heart's for Him, a vacuum only He can fill; some people try to fill that void with relationships, drink, drugs, money, work, etc.; but they're never completely satisfied. The lead singer for the rock group "Boston" was a young man who seemingly had it all . . . success, more money than he could spend, all the women he could want, more friends than he needed, more drink, more drugs, more everything . . . and he committed suicide. He pinned a note to his shirt that read "I am a lonely soul." And apart from God, we all are.

38

"Get down on your knees and thank God you're still on your feet."

Irish proverb

Two similar questions . . .

From Dickie: "Are young people who die before accepting Christ condemned to Hell?"

From Frank: "Are those people who've never heard of Christ going to Hell?

God searches for us. He cares for us and He wants us to know Him. We will be judged according to the truth we have received; we will not be held accountable for what we do not know. The fact is . . . God will reveal Himself to the true seeker. And let's remember this: All who are in Hell, choose it. Without that self-choice, there could be no Hell.

So, forget the notion that God is cruel in sending innocent people to Hell. The last thing God wants is for anyone to perish, He longs for friendship with us all. For God to send someone to Hell that has never heard of Him is an incorrect view of God.

God reveals Himself throughout the world, in nature, in the sky, the stars and all his creations . . . those that seek Him will find Him. If they've never been exposed to the Gospel, that won't keep them from finding God or entering heaven. Romans 1:20 says "For ever since the world was created, people have seen the earth and sky. Through everything God made, they can clearly see his invisible qualities—-his eternal power and divine nature. So, they have no excuse for not knowing God."

We will be judged according to the truth we have received.

39

"The richest people aren't the ones who have the most, they are the ones who need the least."

Ida Elizabeth Townsend

From Mike: "Why do you allow killings and violence throughout the world?"

We must always remember that just as there is a God, there is also a devil. Humanity is not basically good; Evil and violence is the absence of God. God did not create evil, evil is the result of what happens when man does not have God's love present in his heart. God also gave all men "free will" to make their own choices. . . . some men have made truly evil choices. Some men choose to follow the ways of the devil and not God; some people choose Hell over Heaven.

It's okay for us to ask God "Why," as long as we don't get the idea that He owes us an answer. Frankly, God does not owe you or me an explanation. If the Lord did tell you "Why" things happen the way they do; would that ease your pain or heal your broken heart? Probably not, it would, more than likely, even raise more questions.

God says, "My ways are above your ways and my thoughts above yours." God never promised us He would inform us all about His plan ahead of time. He just promised He has one. Life is a tough journey, full of confusion, struggles, and a lot of "I don't knows." However, when we arrive in heaven one day and meet God face to face, then you'll be able to say, "Now I know."

God is mysterious at times, the Bible says "The secret things belong to the Lord." Men will always do evil things because of the influence of the devil and their free will to accept that. All we can do is trust in the Lord and know that His ways are better than ours.

41

"Here's a test to find whether your mission on earth is finished: If you are alive, it isn't"

From Tana: "Do you really exist? If so, why can't we see you?"

He is all around us, every birth is a gift from God; every breath you take is a gift from God. Every mountain and river and sunset you see is a gift from God. He is always with us and will never leave us. Why doesn't He show himself? He has many times. He lived on the earth for 33 years, many people saw Him, they saw many miracles performed by Him, they looked into the face of God, and yet some still didn't believe! Why would you think it would be any different today?

People love the darkness and will rationalize anything in order to continue their sinful lusts and ways of life. As Jesus told Thomas, "Blessed are those who saw me and believed; even more blessed are those who have not seen me and yet still believe."

Did Jesus really exist? Remember, the Romans were experts at death; they crucified thousands upon thousands of people, including Jesus. They knew what they were doing. Jesus died on that cross to pay a debt He didn't owe for us who couldn't pay the debt we did owe. He died for us. Three days later, He rose from the dead, appearing to over 500 people, just as He said He would. Most of his apostles were tortured to try and get confessions that it was all a lie; all they had to do was say "yes, we made it all up, it's not true." But they knew what they had seen was real, they knew they had seen the risen Lord and because of this fact:

Matthew was killed in Ethiopia by a sword wound.

Mark was dragged by horses through the streets of Alexandria, Egypt until he was dead.

Luke was hanged in Greece

John was boiled in huge vats of oil, only to survive this and a lengthy imprisonment to die an old man . . . the only apostle to die peacefully.

Peter was crucified upside down

James was thrown 100 feet off the Temple wall when he refused to deny his faith in Jesus.

James the Great was beheaded

Bartholomew was flayed to death by a whip

Andrew was crucified on an X-shaped cross, after being whipped and beaten . . . he preached for two days while hanging on this cross until he died.

Thomas was stabbed with a spear.

Jude was killed with arrows when he refused to deny his faith in Christ.

Matthias was stoned, then beheaded.

Paul was tortured and then beheaded after a lengthy imprisonment.

All any of these men had to do was deny what they had seen . . . so, to answer your question, "Did He really exist?" Yes, they could not deny the Lord even to save their own lives.

And, how do we explain that one man, Jesus, who died 2000 years ago, has changed the world? That He is still the most influential person in history? That more books and paintings are about Him than all other people combined? Because He lived then, just as He lives now.

42

"We were made by God and for God, and until we figure that out, life isn't going to make any sense.

Rick Warren

From Kali: "Are there angels?" and, "Will cats and dogs be in heaven?"

First, didn't the Lord say that the lion will lay down with the lamb? And, since He created all creatures, why wouldn't He call them all home some day?

Secondly, the Bible references angels hundreds of times, why would the Lord reference them so often if they weren't real? The Bible is not a book where we have to guess what's true or not true; or some kind of puzzle that we have to figure out. It's God's word to us, He cannot and would not lie to us.

Angels straddle both heaven and earth and seemingly, they are created beings who never die. They have special work here on earth for believers; we don't know what they're doing while they're doing it; they just do God's work, take care of business and we are seldom aware of it. I say seldom, because sometimes, maybe we are. Billy Graham said "Angels are God's secret agents." They are doing the work God has called them to do.

The Bible clearly teaches, "The angel of the Lord encamps all around those who fear Him, and delivers them." The Bible also tells us that we "have unwittingly entertained angels." Think about that. I know there are times in our lives when things happen unexpectedly to maybe save us from something bad. It's happened to me and probably you as well. Did I have a guardian angel helping me? Looking out for me? I don't know, I doubt that an angel would tell you he is an angel.

Angels are at work in our lives, protecting us, guiding us, and sometimes even speaking to us. They work undercover and without publicity . . . God's secret agents.

Kali

43

"The three most important things to have are faith, hope and love. But the greatest of them is love."

From Gail: "Is the devil real and is Hell real?"

Yes! The Bible describes Satan as a roaring lion walking about seeking whom he may devour. He never takes a vacation, he never rests. He is a lion constantly pursuing his prey. His is always sizing you up; always looking for a weakness; always looking for a vulnerability of some kind. Jesus called Satan the father of all lies . . . so, if Jesus describes him, he is obviously real.

However, remember, although Satan will tempt you, the Lord will never give you more temptation than you can handle. And we'll all be tempted . . . if Satan was bold enough to try and tempt Jesus three times (as he did), you certainly know you and I will be tempted by him and his demons as well. But, God is faithful, He will not allow us to be tempted above what we are able to cope with; He will always give us a way to escape any temptations. There is always a way out.

The devil is not God's equal. The devil is a powerful spirit being, but he has limitations. He can't be all over the world tempting and harassing everyone at the same time. That's why he employs his vast army of demons . . . remember, when God kicked him out of heaven, he took one third of the fallen angels with him. But don't despair, Jesus prays for you, He is your advocate and speaks in your defense when the evil one tries to slander you before the Father. Jesus will always win . . . He is much stronger than the devil and all his minions.

Hell was not made for people, it was created for the Devil and his angels. It was never God's intention to send a person to Hell. He does everything He can to keep us out of it. But God has given us a free will. We have the ability to choose, and God will not violate that. If you want to go to heaven, then you will go—if you put your faith in Christ. But, if you want to go to Hell, then you will. It is your choice.

Hell is simply one's freely chosen path. If it is what you want, then that is what you will get. God wants you to go to heaven, but He will not force you to; He gives you the choice and it's up to you what you do with that choice.

44

"People are illogical, unreasonable and self-centered. Love them anyway."

Before I end this composition I want to describe the two places I've visited that have left an impression on me. Truly, they are as different as can be imagined, yet quite similar in nature. With each, it's as if I've caught a falling star; there is no mystery; there is only paradox, the incontrovertible union of contradictory truths. Falling stars which melt into vapor as I try to grasp them, falling through my fingers like water, like smoke.

In each, the light is stimulating, exciting, exacting; I feel no temptation to sleep or relax, but rather an opposite effect, which sharpens and heightens vision, touch, hearing, taste and smell. Each existing in and of itself with a clarity that is undimmed by any suggestion of a different realm.

I have a loyalty to each, as each is a paradise to me, or you . . . if you have the eyes to see. Men come and go, civilizations rise and fall, yet the earth remains with it's heartbreaking beauty where there are no hearts to break.

Despite their clarity and simplicity, they each have a veil of mystery . . . motionless and silent with a hint of something unknown, unknowable about to be revealed. Waiting. . . . but waiting for what?

There is something my sensibility cannot assimilate, or hasn't been able to yet; I'm still caught by the golden lure, a prospector for life, condemned, doomed, exalted. Each a riddle that has no answer.

45

"Coincidence is when God chooses to remain anonymous."

And, finally . . .

A few words about and to my lovely wife, Susan. A woman who spoils my friends when they visit, who my aunts and uncles love more than me—because she treats them all so specially. Who would, and does, do anything for anyone whenever they ask, with no thought of her own comfort or feelings. A truly giving and devoted sister, a wonderful daughter, a committed friend to many and a wife that is beyond words or description—I am truly blessed to be married to this beautiful girl.

Susan, this is for you:

If not for you, I couldn't even find the door

I couldn't even see the floor

I'd be sad and blue, if not for you

If not for you, the night would see me wide awake

The day would surely have to break

It would not be new, if not for you

If not for you my sky would fall, rain would gather too

Without your love, I'd be nowhere at all, I'd be lost, if not for you

If not for you, the winter would hold no spring

Couldn't hear a robin sing

I just wouldn't have a clue, if not for you.

The End

Susan

www.ingramcontent.com/pod-product-compliance
Lightning Source LLC
Chambersburg PA
CBHW060840050426
42453CB00008B/766